GO, GO America

America

Dan Yaccarino

Scholastic Press
New York

For my parents, who dragged my brother, sister, and me up and down the Eastern Seaboard against our will. I am just starting to appreciate it!

Dan Yaccarino on the go, go with his sister and brother on a family road trip, circa 1970.

Library of Congress Cataloging-in-Publication Data Yaccarino, Dan. Go, go America / Dan Yaccarino.
p. cm. Includes bibliographical references.
ISBN-10: 0-439-70338-7 (hardcover : alk. paper) 1. U.S. states—Miscellanea—Juvenile literature. 2. United States—Miscellanea—Juvenile literature. 3. United States—Description and travel—Juvenile literature. 4. Curiosities and wonders—United States—Juvenile literature. I. Title. E180.Y24 2008
973—dc22 2007005733
ISBN-13: 978-0-439-70338-3
Printed In Singapore 46   First edition, April 2008
10 9 8 7 6 5 4 3 2 1   08 09 10 11 12

All the laws in this book are on the books, or they were at one time. It is possible that some laws are no longer active. But regardless, most of them are still unbelievable.

The display type was set in EPS Interlock and Chicken Basket. The text type was set in too many fonts to list them all. Art direction by Marijka Kostiw and book design by Kristina Albertson

WARNING:
Many of the facts in
this book are wacky
and outrageous.
Fasten your seatbelt!

At the end of our
Farley family road trip,
you can find even more
information about the
U.S.A. Just turn to
pages 72–80.

May I have your
attention, please?

Cluck! Cluck!

Oink! Oink!

Happy
reading!

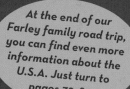

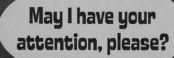

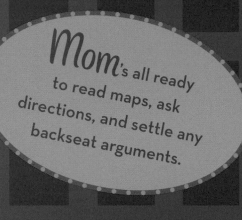

Mom's all ready to read maps, ask directions, and settle any backseat arguments.

Dad can't wait to hit the road! Unfortunately, he's not the greatest driver in the world and has a lousy sense of direction.

Freddie knows lots of interesting facts about the United States and is eager to share his knowledge, even if no one wants to hear it.

MAINE
Pine Tree State

AUGUSTA ★

Almost 40 million pounds of **LOBSTER** is caught off the coast of Maine. That's 90% of all of the delicious lobster eaten in the United States!

Pass the drawn butter, please!

Maine is the only state in the United States whose name has one syllable! Fascinating!

West Quoddy Head Lighthouse is the most easterly point in the U.S.

Did you know . . .

that Farmington is the **EARMUFF** capital of the world? Fifteen-year-old Chester Greenwood came up with the idea while ice-skating in 1873.

THANK GOODNESS!

More **TOOTHPICKS** are produced in Maine than in any other state— around 100 million a day!

You'll need them after eating all that lobster.

90% of the **BLUEBERRIES** in the United States come from Maine, so save some room for dessert!

TABLE OF CONTENTS

NEW HAMPSHIRE
Granite State

The first free public library was the Dublin Juvenile Library, established in 1822.

One of the oldest covered **BRIDGES** in the United States is the Haverhill-Bath Covered Bridge, built in 1829.

CONCORD

Did you know . . .

that Levi Hutchins of Concord invented the first **ALARM CLOCK** in 1787, much to the dismay of roosters everywhere.

The alarm time was not adjustable, so it only rang at 4 AM!

Native New Hampshirite Sarah Josepha Hale wrote "Mary Had a Little Lamb," published in 1830.

The very first **POTATO** planted in the United States was in New Hampshire in 1719.

Hang on!

The highest **WIND SPEED** recorded at ground level was on April 12, 1934, at Mount Washington. The winds were faster than a Category Five hurricane—231 miles per hour!

9

MASSACHUSETTS
Bay State

that the Boston Harbor Light Station, the first U.S. **LIGHTHOUSE**, was lit for the first time on September 14, 1716.

I think I dropped the soap a few blocks back.

Sleeping in your **DAY CLOTHING** is against the law in Boston.

This is your third bath this week, ma'am. You're coming with us.

But doesn't she smell nice!

In 1957, Leominster became the birthplace of the **PLASTIC** lawn flamingo.

An old Boston law states that no one shall take more than one **BATH** per week.

No lawn is complete without one!

BASKETBALL was invented by James Naismith in Springfield in 1891. He taught physical education and wanted an indoor sport for his students during the cold winter months.

Construction started on the nation's first subway in Boston on March 28, 1895.

Hey, did you know, in Marblehead it is illegal to cross the street on Sunday unless it is absolutely necessary.

Have a cookie and a slice!

The chocolate chip cookie, first baked by Ruth Wake in 1930, is the official state cookie of Massachusetts.

The official state **DESSERT** of Massachusetts is Boston cream pie.

The first newspaper published in the American colonies, Publick Occurrences Both Foreign and Domestick, was launched in Boston in 1690.

In Holyoke in 1895, William Morgan invented Mintonette— known today as **VOLLEYBALL.**

At the Boston University Bridge on Commonwealth Avenue you just might see a boat sail **UNDER** a train driving **UNDER** a car moving **UNDER** an airplane.

Now how about that?

VERMONT
Green Mountain State

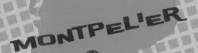
MONTPELIER

Vermont cows produce more than 2.5 billion pounds of milk per year!

How many of them give chocolate milk?

Vermont has the highest ratio of dairy **COWS** to people in the country. One cow per four people.

PEE-YEW!

Did you know . . . that Montpelier has been the official home of the International **ROTTEN SNEAKER CONTEST** since 1975.

Skiing is the single most important tourist industry in the state.

Vermont is known for its great **SKIING.** And thanks to Robert Royce, the first ski tow towed skiers in Woodstock on January 28, 1934.

Vermont produces more **MAPLE SYRUP** than any other state: 500,000 gallons a year!

Pancakes, anyone?

It takes 40 gallons of sap to make 1 gallon of syrup!

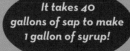

Lake Champlain, not Champagne, dear.

Oops!

MEET THE FABULOUS FARLEY FAMILY!

Follow Mom, Dad, Freddie, Fran, and Fido on their fun fact-filled journey from Maine to Hawaii as they discover our weird and wondrous United States of America!

Fran would prefer to be biking, hiking, or skiing cross-country rather than riding in a car. And she's still mad at Mom for telling her that she can't ride on the roof.

Beware of **BIGFOOT**! He lurks throughout the states and in these pages. Can you spot him?

Fido thinks they are going to the park.

WASHINGTON
67

OREGON
66

IDAHO
60

MONTANA
58

NORTH DAKOTA
57

SOUTH DAKOTA
56

NEVADA
61

WYOMING
59

NEBRASKA
49

CALIFORNIA
64

UTAH
62

COLORADO
55

KANSAS
50

ARIZONA
63

NEW MEXICO
54

OKLAHOMA
51

TEXAS
52

ALASKA
68

The first traffic law in the American colonies was created in 1678, when authorities did not allow horses to gallop on local streets in Newport.

The first speeding ticket was given in Newport in 1904.

Dear, maybe you should slow down.

PROVIDENCE

Did you know . . . that the longest **BASEBALL** game in history — played between the New York Rochester Redwings and the Rhode Island Pawtucket Red Sox — started on April 18, 1981, and ended 65 days, 21 hours, and 16 minutes later on June 23, 1981.

(No, they didn't actually play that whole time!)

BOP ON DOWN
to the Newport Jazz Festival.
Founded in 1954, **DADDY-O.**

Be sure to make the scene!

Rhode Island is the smallest state — only 1,545 square miles!

The first **CIRCUS** in the United States was in Newport in 1774!

The Flying Horse Carousel in Watch Hill is believed to be the oldest continually operating **CAROUSEL** in the country. Built in 1867, it was left after a traveling carnival could no longer transport it.

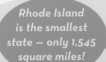

NEW YORK
Empire State

ALBANY

TO U.S.A.
LOVE, FRANCE

TOOT!
TOOT!

Did you know . . .

that on October 28, 1886, the people of **FRANCE** gave the Statue of Liberty to the people of the United States.

It says here that George Washington took his oath as president on the balcony at Federal Hall in 1789.

Joseph Gayetty of New York City produced the first packaged **TOILET PAPER** in 1857.

Thank goodness.

Can you pass the mustard?

Thousands of fans turn out for Nathan's Famous international **HOT DOG–EATING CONTEST** every July 4 at the original Nathan's in Coney Island.

Manhattan's Astor Theater showed the first **3-D FILMS** to a paying audience on June 10, 1915.

14

Annie Taylor, a 63-year-old retired schoolteacher, was the first person to go over Niagara Falls **IN A BARREL** on October 24, 1901. Don't try this at home, kids!

The original King Kong movie was made in 1933.

The first capital of the United States was New York City.

The Empire State, dear. Not umpire.

Be sure to visit the Kazoo Factory and Museum in Eden. It's the only metal kazoo factory left in the world.

Completed in 1931, the **EMPIRE STATE BUILDING** is 1,453 feet and 8 9/16 inches to the top of the lightning rod, and has 103 floors, 6,500 windows, and 1,860 steps from street level to the 103rd floor.

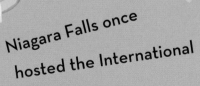

Niagara Falls once hosted the International **JUGGLERS** Festival.

In New York, it is against the law to **THROW** a ball at someone's head for fun.

CONNECTICUT
Constitution State

HARTFORD

The world's first telephone directory, a sheet of paper with 50 names on it, came out February 21, 1878, in New Haven.

Be sure to visit the **NUT** Museum in Old Lyme.

It says here that you are what you eat.

Do I look like a pig? Woof!

Did you know . . .

that cattle branding in the States began in Connecticut when state law called for farmers to mark all of their **PIGS.**

No one can fly a kite on the streets of Danbury without a permit from the mayor.

The nation's first **HAMBURGERS** were served in New Haven at Louis' Lunch Sandwich Shop in 1895. Louis Lassen sold steak sandwiches, and because he didn't like to waste the excess beef from his daily lunch rush, he ground it up, grilled it, and served it between two slices of bread — and America's first hamburger was created!

Now who's hungry?

It is illegal in Hartford to cross the street while **WALKING ON YOUR HANDS.**

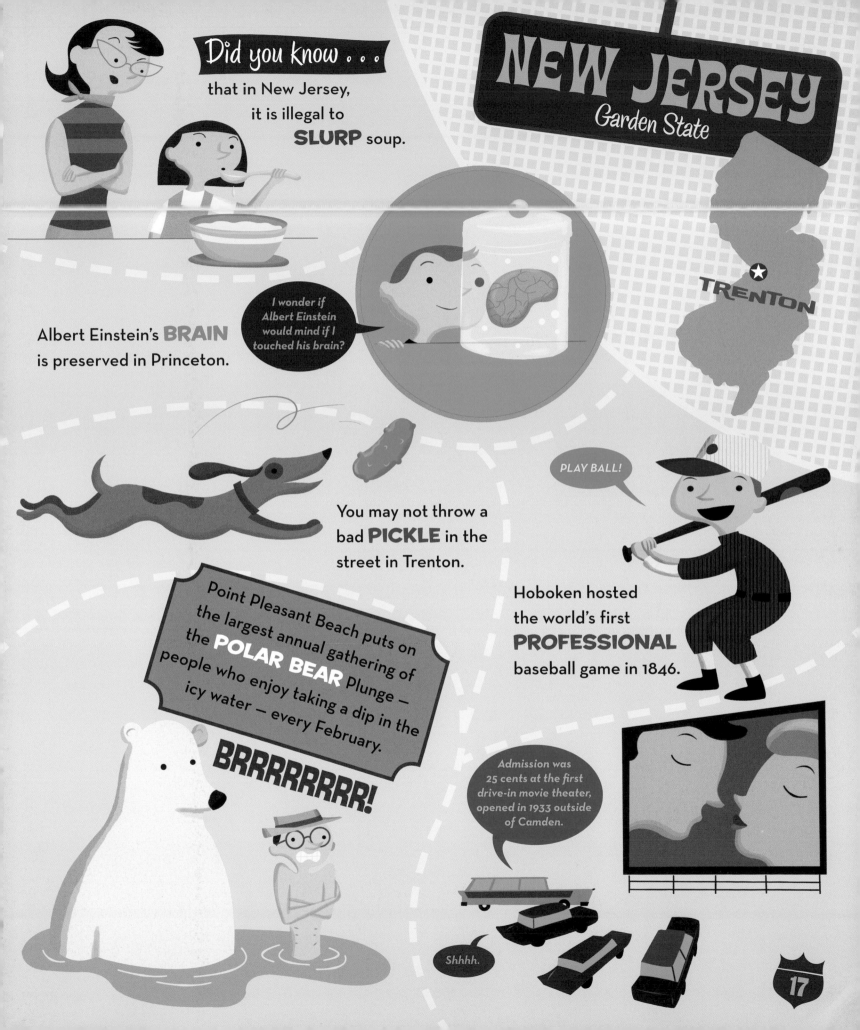

Did you know . . .

that in New Jersey, it is illegal to **SLURP** soup.

NEW JERSEY
Garden State

TRENTON

I wonder if Albert Einstein would mind if I touched his brain?

Albert Einstein's **BRAIN** is preserved in Princeton.

You may not throw a bad **PICKLE** in the street in Trenton.

PLAY BALL!

Hoboken hosted the world's first **PROFESSIONAL** baseball game in 1846.

Point Pleasant Beach puts on the largest annual gathering of the **POLAR BEAR** Plunge — people who enjoy taking a dip in the icy water — every February.

BRRRRRRRR!

Admission was 25 cents at the first drive-in movie theater, opened in 1933 outside of Camden.

Shhhh.

17

PENNSYLVANIA
Keystone State

HARRISBURG ★

Each February 2, national attention is on Punxsutawney, where a **GROUNDHOG'S** shadow will predict the number of weeks remaining in winter.

Any requests?

Yum!

After raising two kids, wrestling is a piece of cake.

In Philadelphia, **WRESTLERS** can be fined for throwing their opponents out of the ring.

Every May, Millersville hosts International Tuba Day, a gathering of **TUBA** enthusiasts. Earplugs are optional.

The first commercial broadcasting station in the world was KDKA in Pittsburgh, which aired on November 2, 1920.

Hershey is considered the **CHOCOLATE CAPITAL OF THE WORLD** (and the site of the world's largest chocolate factory)!

The nation's largest insectarium is in Philadelphia. Watch **TARANTULAS, COCKROACHES,** and **ASSORTED BUGS.**

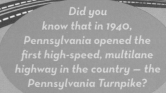

Did you know that in 1940, Pennsylvania opened the first high-speed, multilane highway in the country — the Pennsylvania Turnpike?

The Philadelphia Zoo is the oldest zoo in the country. It was chartered in 1859 but, due to the Civil War, didn't open to the public until 1874.

But, Dad, I didn't do it!

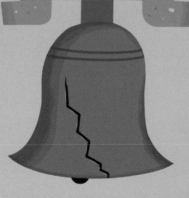

Did you know . . .
that since 1752, Philadelphia has been home to the **LIBERTY BELL.**

Pittsburgh has 44,645 **STEPS!** Stacked on top of one another, they'd be over 24,000 feet high. That's higher than most of the Himalayan Mountains! Pittsburgh has 712 city staircases.

Whew!

DELAWARE
First State

At Rehoboth Beach, no person shall pretend to sleep on a bench along the boardwalk.

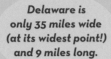

Delaware is only 35 miles wide (at its widest point!) and 9 miles long.

What is . . . 10 feet in diameter and holds 180 gallons of oil and 800 **CHICKEN** quarters? A frying pan built in 1950 for the Delmarva Chicken Festival!

Sussex County raises more than 200 million broiler chickens a year—that's the most of any county in the U.S.!

So who wants a drumstick?

Delaware was the first state to formally approve the U.S. Constitution.

In 1880, the first beauty contest in the United States — **"MISS UNITED STATES"** — was held in Rehoboth Beach. Thomas Edison was a judge.

Did you know . . .

that in Sussex County at the World Championship **PUNKIN CHUNKIN** event, folks use catapults, cannons, and a variety of human-powered gadgets to see just how far they can launch a single pumpkin!

Someone once launched a pumpkin more than 4,000 feet!

It's out of this world!

Jet on over to the most visited museum in the world, the **National Air and Space Museum.**

WASHINGTON, D.C.

It's not a state, but what's a trip through the U.S.A. without a visit to our nation's capital?

Washington, D.C. is the home of the National **SPELLING BEE** finals . . .

. . . and the National Geography Bee!

The National Cherry Blossom Festival celebrates 3,000 Japanese cherry trees — a **GIFT** from Japan to the United States in 1912.

Did you know . . .

that there is an International **SPY** Museum? It's the only **SPY** museum in the United States all about **SPYING.**

Keep it hush-hush!

Do you think they saw us?

D.C. is home to the **SQUISHED** Penny Museum. Their entire collection is worth about 50 dollars. Now that's a lot of pennies!

MARYLAND
Old Line State

ANNAPOLIS

On June 24, 1784, thirteen-year-old Edward Warren flew above Baltimore, in the first successful manned **BALLOON** launch in the United States.

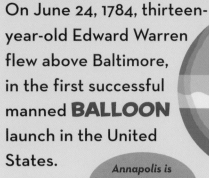

Annapolis is known as America's Sailing Capital.

King William's **SCHOOL,** one of the first schools in the United States, opened in 1696.

Wake up! It's time for school!

What's school?

During the War of 1812, at Baltimore's Fort McHenry, the **AMERICAN FLAG** withstood a 25-hour bombardment by the British, inspiring Francis Scott Key to write "The Star-Spangled Banner."

Did you know . . .

that Baltimore hosts the annual Chicken **CLUCKING** Contest every June and the annual Hog Calling Contest every July.

CLUCK! CLUCK!

In 1828, Baltimore became home to the nation's first umbrella factory.

Harve de Grace is the Decoy Capital of the World.

Did you find Dad's keys yet?

Thomas Moore invented the first **REFRIGERATOR** in Baltimore in 1803.

Honest, Dad, it wasn't me!

Virginia is famous for its **BLUE** Ridge Mountains.

VIRGINIA
Old Dominion State

RICHMOND

Did you know . . .

that the Mid-Atlantic **HERMIT CRAB** Challenge in Virginia Beach features the Miss Curvaceous Crustacean Beauty Pageant, where hermit crabs show off their decorated shells.

George Washington, Thomas Jefferson, James Madison, James Monroe, William Henry Harrison, John Tyler, Zachary Taylor, and Woodrow Wilson.

Virginia holds the record as the **BIRTHPLACE** of the most U.S. presidents.

In Prince William County, **PETS** may not trespass. They must be kept on a leash. It's the law.

The first theater in the U.S. was opened in Williamsburg in 1776. Bravo!

Is it 8 AM yet?

In Norfolk, hens cannot lay **EGGS** before 8 AM or after 4 PM.

It is illegal to **TICKLE** a girl in Norton.

Tee! Hee!

How should I know? I'm a chicken.

23

NORTH CAROLINA
Tar Heel State

The self-kicking—OUCH!—machine outside of—OUCH!—New Bern was constructed by Tom Haywood. OUCH! Just turn your backside to the boots and move the crank! OUCH!!!!

OUCH!

I didn't know that North Carolina was below South Carolina.

You've got the map upside down, dear.

Fran, did you know that there are almost 400 species of birds at the Pea Island National Wildlife Refuge on Hatteras Island?

Freddie, did you know that there's a bird on your head?

Fights between
CATS AND DOGS
are prohibited in Barber.

The **VENUS FLYTRAP** grows naturally only in North and South Carolina.

The world's largest flying American flag is in Gastonia. Visible for 30 miles, it's 7,410 square feet, 65 feet tall, 114 feet wide, and 180 pounds!

 that Morehead City hosts the annual **BALD** Is Beautiful Convention.

24

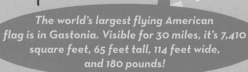

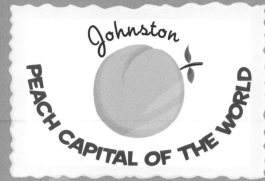

Johnston

PEACH CAPITAL OF THE WORLD

SOUTH CAROLINA
Palmetto State

COLUMBIA

★ START

Every May, Aiken holds its annual **LOBSTER** races.

All lobsters to the line.

Lake Murray is home to a water **MONSTER** that was first spotted in 1933.

Did you know . . .

that the South Carolina **POULTRY FESTIVAL** happens every May in Batesburg-Leesville.

COCK-A-DOODLE-DOO!

This is fun!

The state **DANCE** of South Carolina is the shag.

Fort Sumter in Charleston Harbor is where the American Civil War began on April 12, 1861.

Charleston is famous for having some of the country's oldest graveyards and, not surprisingly, lots of **HAUNTED** sites.

25

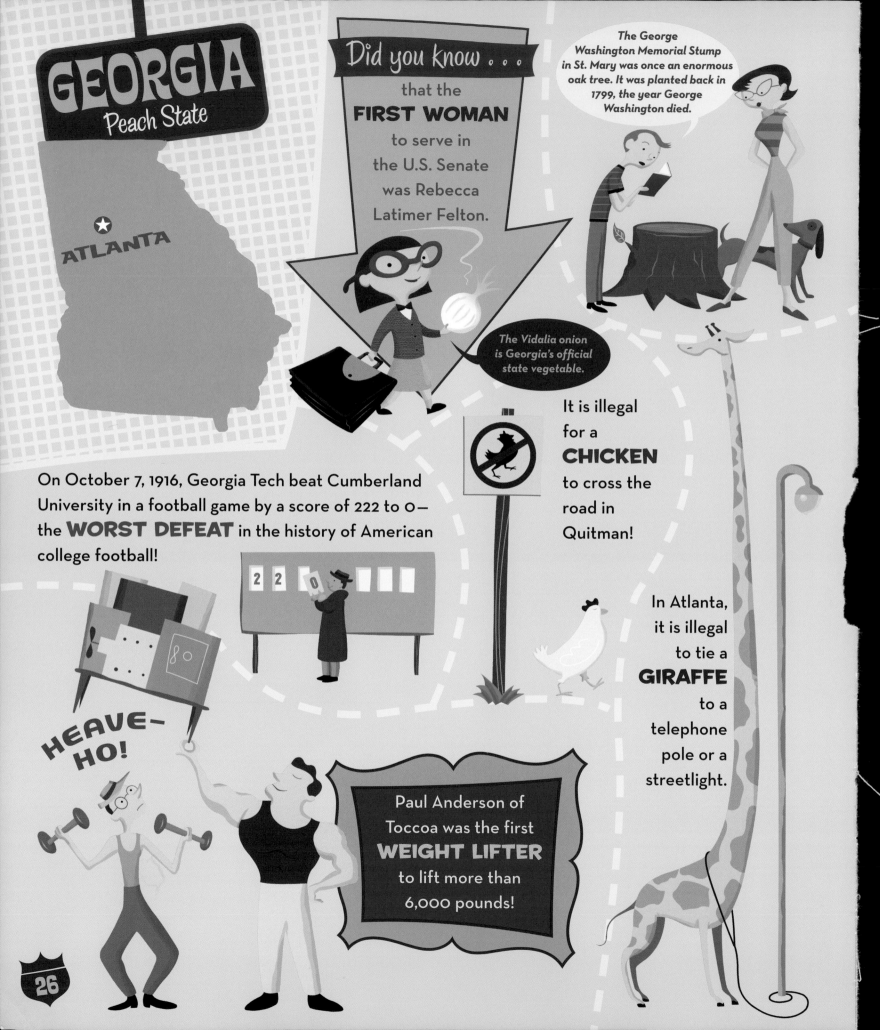

GEORGIA
Peach State

ATLANTA ★

Did you know . . . that the **FIRST WOMAN** to serve in the U.S. Senate was Rebecca Latimer Felton.

The George Washington Memorial Stump in St. Mary was once an enormous oak tree. It was planted back in 1799, the year George Washington died.

The Vidalia onion is Georgia's official state vegetable.

It is illegal for a **CHICKEN** to cross the road in Quitman!

On October 7, 1916, Georgia Tech beat Cumberland University in a football game by a score of 222 to 0—the **WORST DEFEAT** in the history of American college football!

In Atlanta, it is illegal to tie a **GIRAFFE** to a telephone pole or a streetlight.

HEAVE-HO!

Paul Anderson of Toccoa was the first **WEIGHT LIFTER** to lift more than 6,000 pounds!

ALABAMA
Yellowhammer State

Did you know . . . that Huntsville, nicknamed Rocket City, is home to the Redstone Arsenal and the U.S. Space and **ROCKET CENTER.**

Kids can build a rocket at the Space Camp in Huntsville.

Hang on!

MONTGOMERY

In Alabama, books about outlaws are outlawed.

The world's first electric trolley system was introduced in 1886 in Montgomery.

The World's Largest Chair—at 33 feet tall!—sits in Anniston.

Sock it to me!

Okay, dear.

With an estimated 76 million pairs of **SOCKS** produced a year in Fort Payne, no wonder it's the sock capital of the world.

The Boll Weevil Monument in Enterprise honors the **BUGS** that forced Alabama farmers to grow peanuts (a more profitable crop) rather than cotton.

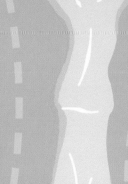

27

FLORIDA
Sunshine State

Has anyone seen the keys?

Right here, Dad.

Visitors and residents enjoy collecting prehistoric **SHARKS' TEETH** in Venice, which is known as the shark tooth capital of the world.

Tampa hosts the National **PUPPETRY** Festival.

Florida is the only state that has two rivers with the same name: Withlacoochee!

The Overseas Highway, which runs from Miami to Key West, is one of the longest over-water roads in the world.

In Miami on June 1, 1937, Amelia Earhart took off in her airplane in hopes that she'd be the first woman to fly around the world. She never made it. Her disappearance is an unsolved mystery even today.

28

Key West hosts an annual **UNDERWATER** Music Festival.

Yum!

At the Fellsmere **FROG LEG** Festival, 80,000 frog-leg eaters come to eat more than 6,000 pounds of frog!

Clearwater is the U.S. city with the highest rate of **LIGHTNING STRIKES.**

Did you know . . .

that Florida is known as the Alligator State and has the world's largest **ALLIGATOR** population.

Alligator Wrestling

People Wrestling

Ed Leeds Kalnin single-handedly built the castle in Florida City in 1936, but later relocated it to Homestead.

Homestead is the home of the **CORAL CASTLE,** a castle built with more than 1,100 tons of coral rock.

He moved the entire castle by himself! No one really knows how he did it.

29

MISSISSIPPI
Magnolia State

The Mississippi River, aka Old Man River, is our nation's chief waterway.

JACKSON

Cheers! Cheers!

ROOT BEER was invented in Biloxi in 1898 by Edward Adolf Barq, Sr.

While on a hunting expedition in Sharkey County in 1902, President Theodore Roosevelt refused to shoot a captured bear cub, which inspired a cartoon strip, which led to the creation of the world-famous **TEDDY BEAR.**

Gulf coast, dear.

Oops!

Did you know . . . that Petal is home to the International **CHECKER** Hall of Fame.

King me.

30

Safety first!

In New Orleans, a fire engine must **STOP** for a red light, even if it is on its way to a fire.

LOUISIANA
Pelican State

★ BATON ROUGE

Buzz! Buzz!

The HONEYBEE is Louisiana's official state insect.

DON'T MISS IT!

The Battle of New Orleans, which made Andrew Jackson a national hero, was fought two weeks after the War of 1812 had ended. (It took more than a month for the news of the war's end to reach Louisiana.)

Gueydan is known as the **DUCK CAPITAL** of America.

Did you know . . . that New Orleans's annual Mardi Gras celebration is a colorful **CARNIVAL** filled with music, food, and costumes.

It is illegal to steal an **ALLIGATOR** in Louisiana.

31

ARKANSAS
Natural State

★ LITTLE ROCK

If you wash my back, I'll wash yours.

In Arkansas, **ALLIGATORS** may not be kept in bathtubs.

IN NORTH LITTLE ROCK, A CITY LAW SAYS THAT A PERSON MAY NOT SCREAM, SHOUT, OR SING ON THE STREET.

Don't miss Atkins's annual **PICKLEFEST** every May.

Did you know . . .
that in Little Rock it is against the law for dogs to **BARK** after 6 PM.

ARF! WOOF! BOWWOW!

The Purplehull Pea Festival is held every June in Emerson.

And don't miss the garden tiller races or the pea-shelling contest!

Stuttgart holds the World Championship **DUCK CALLING CONTEST.**

Arkansas must be pronounced "Arkansaw." It's the law—mispronounce it and you just might be arrested.

Crater of Diamonds State Park is the only place in the world where people can keep the gems they find. An average of two **DIAMONDS** per day are unearthed!

32

Even though he died in 1940, Robert Pershing Wadlow of Alton is still the **TALLEST MAN**, at 8 feet, 11.1 inches tall.

THAT IS MIGHTY TALL!

The first successful **PARACHUTE JUMP** made from a moving airplane was performed by Captain Albert Berry in St. Louis on March 12, 1912.

Look out below!

The world's largest pecan can be seen at the George James Pecan Museum in Brunswick. It's 12,000 pounds!

The first well-documented case of **RAINING FROGS** fell from the Kansas City skies in 1873.

At the 1904 World's Fair in St. Louis, an ice cream vendor ran out of cups and asked a **WAFFLE** vendor to roll up waffles to hold the ice cream. Thus, the ice cream cone was born!

By the time he died in 1910, his whiskers had grown to 12 feet, 6 inches!

Did you know . . . that in 1860, Pike County resident Valentine Tapley swore that if Lincoln were elected, he would never **SHAVE.**

33

TENNESSEE
Volunteer State

★ NASHVILLE

Ribbit Ribbit

In Memphis, frogs are prohibited to **CROAK** after 11 PM.

Did you know . . .

that Nashville's *Grand Ole Opry* is the oldest continual **RADIO** program in the United States.

The first broadcast was on November 28, 1925.

Visit Craighead Caverns in Sweetwater and discover **THE LOST SEA,** an 800 foot by 220 foot underground lake.

In Knoxville, it's against the law to lasso a fish.

Where can you see a 1947 GMC **"BUBBLENOSE"** wrecker and a 1919 three-ton crane? The International Towing and Recovery Hall of Fame Museum in Chattanooga!

Grab a plate of catfish at the World's Biggest Fish Fry in Paris (no, not France), where more than 12,500 pounds are served up!

Grrrr...

CATFISH

Chattanooga is home to the Tennessee Aquarium, the world's largest freshwater aquarium, which holds 400,000 gallons of water. And watch out for the **TEN-FOOT SHARKS!**

Fore!

TOM THUMB, the first miniature golf course, was built in Chattanooga.

Knoxville gained the nickname **"THE MARBLE CITY"** in the early 1900s, thanks to all its quarries and its Tennessee Pink Marble.

And away we go!

Visit Elvis Presley's beloved home, **GRACELAND,** in Memphis.

KENTUCKY
Bluegrass State

★ **FRANKFORT**

The song **"HAPPY BIRTHDAY TO YOU"** was written by two Louisville sisters in 1893.

You got your wish.

The largest amount of **GOLD** stored anywhere in the world is held in the underground vaults of Fort Knox. The stash is worth more than 100 billion dollars!

Catch the Louisville Slugger Museum and Factory, well marked by the world's **BIGGEST BASEBALL BAT!**

This grass isn't blue.

Kentucky **BLUEGRASS** was brought to the United States by the early colonists from Europe, northern Asia, and the mountains of Algeria and Morocco.

Kentucky lays claim to the invention of the **CHEESEBURGER** (and so do Colorado and California. Hmmm.)

Did you know . . .

that the Kentucky Derby is the country's oldest continually held **HORSE RACE?** It is run at Churchill Downs in Louisville.

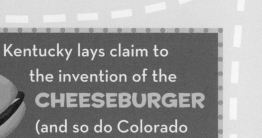

And that's straight from the horse's mouth!

At 71 years old, Kentucky-born Alben W. Barkley was the oldest U.S. vice president when he assumed office in 1949.

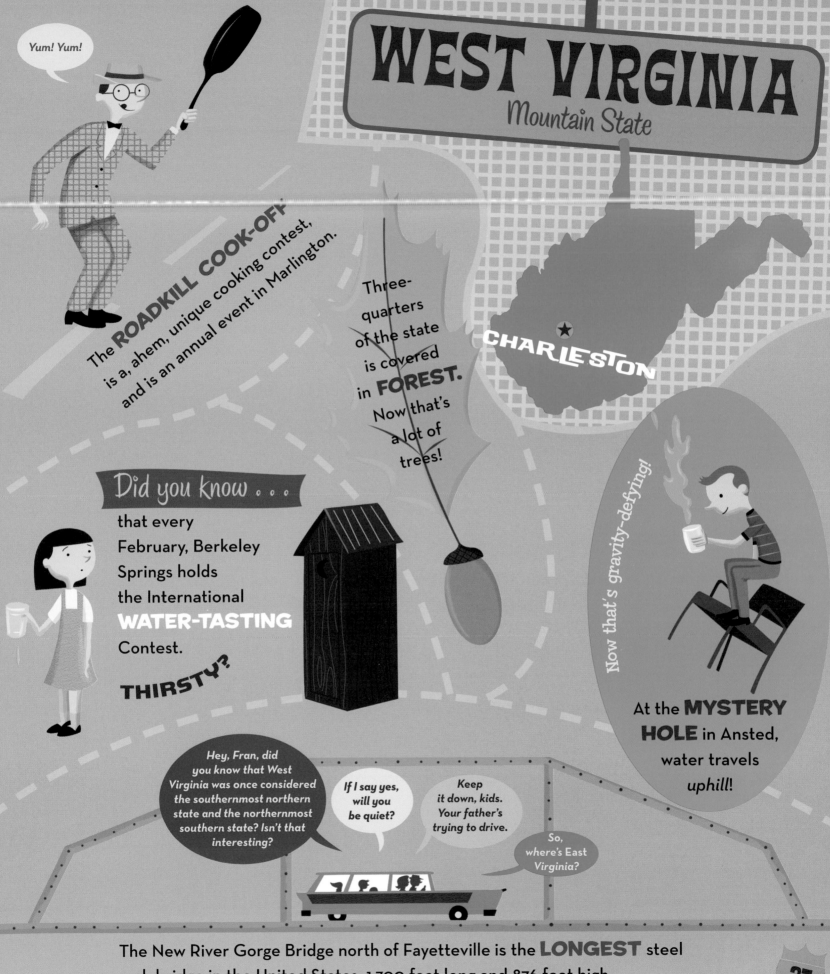

WEST VIRGINIA
Mountain State

Yum! Yum!

The **ROADKILL COOK-OFF** is a, ahem, unique cooking contest, and is an annual event in Marlington.

Three-quarters of the state is covered in **FOREST**. Now that's a lot of trees!

CHARLESTON

Did you know . . . that every February, Berkeley Springs holds the International **WATER-TASTING** Contest. **THIRSTY?**

Now that's gravity-defying!

At the **MYSTERY HOLE** in Ansted, water travels *uphill!*

Hey, Fran, did you know that West Virginia was once considered the southernmost northern state and the northernmost southern state? Isn't that interesting?

If I say yes, will you be quiet?

Keep it down, kids. Your father's trying to drive.

So, where's East Virginia?

The New River Gorge Bridge north of Fayetteville is the **LONGEST** steel arch bridge in the United States: 1,700 feet long and 876 feet high.

OHIO
Buckeye State

C'mon, Fran! There are so many exciting sites to visit in Columbus! They have the Accounting Hall of Fame and the Drainage Hall of Fame!

What a swell city!

The **FIRST** ambulance service in the country was established in Cincinnati in 1865.

In Youngstown, people are **FORBIDDEN** to ride on the roof of a taxicab!

In Cincinnati, the nation's **FIRST** professional city fire department began operation on April 1, 1853.

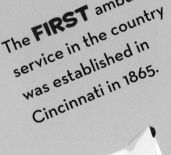

Did you know . . .

that Clarence Crane invented Life Savers in Cleveland in 1912. The **CANDY,** not the life preserver.

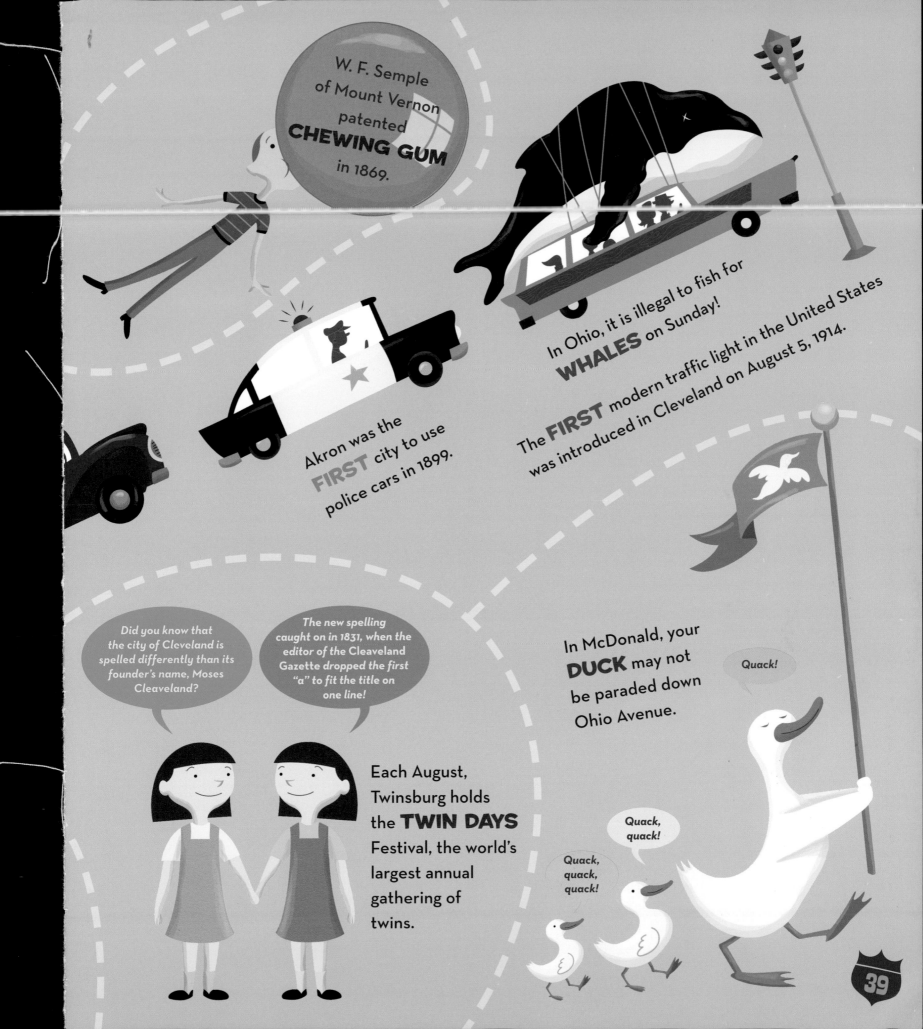

W. F. Semple of Mount Vernon patented **CHEWING GUM** in 1869.

In Ohio, it is illegal to fish for **WHALES** on Sunday!

The **FIRST** modern traffic light in the United States was introduced in Cleveland on August 5, 1914.

Akron was the **FIRST** city to use police cars in 1899.

Did you know that the city of Cleveland is spelled differently than its founder's name, Moses Cleaveland?

The new spelling caught on in 1831, when the editor of the Cleaveland Gazette dropped the first "a" to fit the title on one line!

In McDonald, your **DUCK** may not be paraded down Ohio Avenue.

Each August, Twinsburg holds the **TWIN DAYS** Festival, the world's largest annual gathering of twins.

Quack!

Quack, quack!

Quack, quack, quack!

39

INDIANA
Hoosier State

★ INDIANAPOLIS

E-I-E-I-O!

Since 1899, Martinsville has been home to the first successful **GOLDFISH** farm in the United States.

Since 1911, Indianapolis has been home to the Indy 500!

START YOUR ENGINES!

F

Every year, Santa Claus, Indiana, receives thousands of letters for **SANTA!**

Ho! Ho! Ho!

Five men from Indiana have been elected as vice presidents: Schuyler Colfax, Thomas A. Hendricks, Charles W. Fairbanks, Thomas Marshall, and Dan Quayle.

The world's first **TRANSISTOR RADIO** was made in Indianapolis in 1954, manufactured by Regency Electronics.

And now, back to our regularly scheduled program. . . .

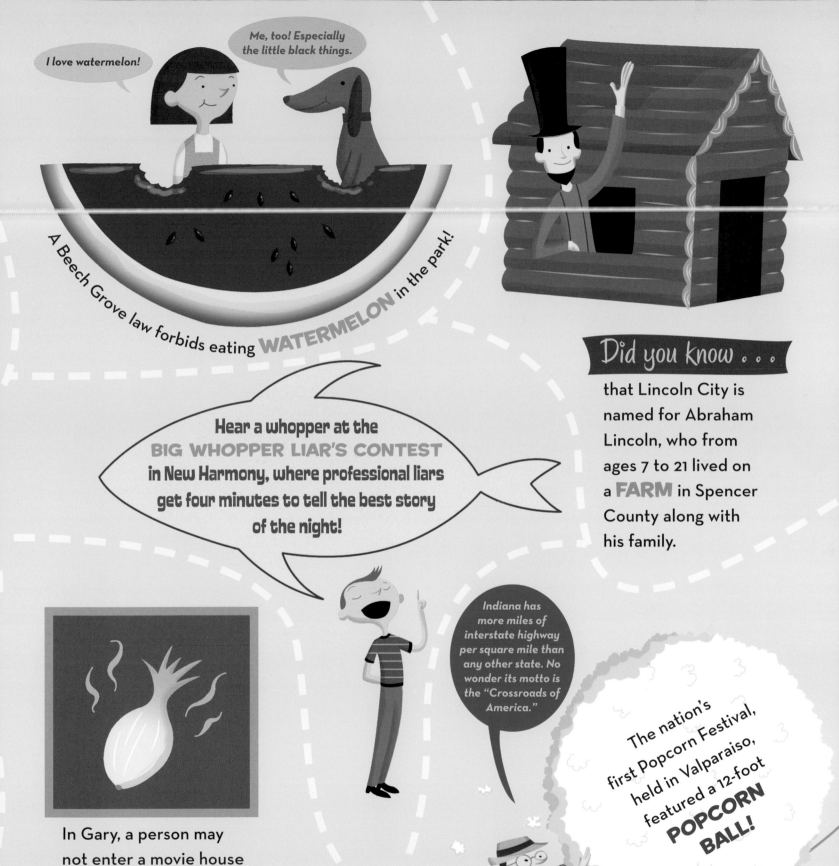

I love watermelon!

Me, too! Especially the little black things.

A Beech Grove law forbids eating **WATERMELON** in the park!

Hear a whopper at the **BIG WHOPPER LIAR'S CONTEST** in New Harmony, where professional liars get four minutes to tell the best story of the night!

Did you know . . .

that Lincoln City is named for Abraham Lincoln, who from ages 7 to 21 lived on a **FARM** in Spencer County along with his family.

Indiana has more miles of interstate highway per square mile than any other state. No wonder its motto is the "Crossroads of America."

In Gary, a person may not enter a movie house or theater or ride a public streetcar within four hours of eating garlic. **IT'S THE LAW!**

The nation's first Popcorn Festival, held in Valparaiso, featured a 12-foot **POPCORN BALL!**

MICHIGAN
Wolverine State

★ LANSING

Eau Claire holds the International **CHERRY PIT AND SPIT** Competition every July.

MOTOWN RECORDS was founded in Detroit by Berry Gordy, Jr., in 1959, and named after the city's nickname — Motor Town.

Ginger ale was created accidentally in 1866 in Detroit. James Vernor returned from the Civil War to find that a beverage **CONCOCTION** he'd stored in an oak case four years earlier had turned a delicious gingery flavor.

Did you know . . . that Colon is known as the **MAGIC** capital of the world.

ABRACADABRA! ALAKAZAM!

STOP

The first stop sign appeared in Detroit in 1915.

Detroiters were the first people in the nation to receive assigned phone numbers in 1879.

Battle Creek makes more breakfast cereal than any other place in the world.

Each June, at the **CEREAL FESTIVAL** in Battle Creek, more than 300 six-foot-long tables are set up to create the World's Longest Breakfast Table for 60,000 attendees.

Wisconsin has more than 14,000 lakes and 7,446 streams and rivers. If you stuck them end to end, they'd stretch nearly 27,000 miles — enough to circle the whole planet!

WOW-WEE!

WISCONSIN
Badger State

The **SPINNING TOP** Museum in Burlington exhibits more than 2,000 tops, yo-yos, and gyroscopes. *It'll make your head spin!*

In Wisconsin, all boarding-houses, clubs, hotels, and restaurants are required to serve at least two-thirds of an ounce of cheese with every meal sold at 25 cents or more. Mmmm . . . Limburger cheese.

Wisconsin is known as America's dairy land.

Stink-a-licious!

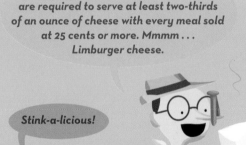

Wisconsin's 1.6 million dairy **COWS** produce 15 percent of the nation's milk and more than 350 varieties of cheese.

Did you know . . .

that in Ashland, boys are forbidden to play **MARBLES** — if they play for keeps.

Oh, no! I lost my marbles!

In 1960, Bloomer P.E. teacher Wally Mohrman decided to create a contest for speed jumping. Now Bloomer's the **ROPE JUMP** capital of the world!

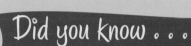

43

MINNESOTA
North Star State

ST. PAUL

678, 679, 680 . . .

What are you counting, Freddie?

I heard that Minnesota is the land of 10,000 lakes, and I'm just making sure!

You stink!

In Minneapolis, it is unlawful to tease or torment SKUNKS!

In Pine Island, it is illegal for a man to pass a cow without **TIPPING** his hat.

Where are your manners?

Were you talking to me?

TRICK OR TREAT!

Trick or treat, smell my feet. Give me something good to eat!

Anoka is the **HALLOWEEN** capital of the world!

44

that McGraw Electric Company of Minneapolis marketed the first automatic POP-UP toaster — the Toastmaster — in 1926.

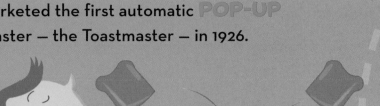

WANTED!

The Land of 10,000 Lakes declares **MOSQUITOES** a public nuisance by law!

New York Mills is home to the Great American **THINK-OFF CONTEST.** Deploy all thinking caps!

Come to Lac qui Parle State Park and see a 3.6-billion-year-old rock called gneiss (pronounced "nice"). You'll see some of the oldest rocks in the world!

Legend has it that the enormous footprints of Paul Bunyan and his faithful ox, Babe, created Minnesota's 10,000 lakes.

PAUL BUNYAN'S grave can been seen in Keliher, where his epitaph reads:

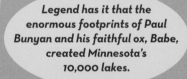

Here lies Paul, and that's all.

45

ILLINOIS
Prairie State

Thousands make the leap every year at the World **FREE FALL** Convention in Rantoul—with parachutes, of course.

SPRINGFIELD

Geronimo!

In Illinois, there are a million and a half acres of water for fishing.

Lincoln Park Zoo is more than 100 years old and is home to more than 1,000 animals, including giraffes!

Hey, Fran, Illinois has more units of local government than any other state! More than 6,000! I betcha didn't know that! Didja? Huh? Huh?

Arcola is the **BROOM CORN** capital of the world.

The Chicago River is dyed **GREEN** on Saint Patrick's Day.

Stop Illinois-ing me, Freddie!

Have a sweeping good time!

Mendotta is home to the annual STA-BIL National **LAWN MOWER** Races. **START YOUR ENGINES . . .**

Got a cookie?

In Kenilworth, a rooster must step back 300 feet from any residence when he wishes to crow. Hens that wish to cackle must step back 200 feet from any residence.

Did you know...

that since 1942, Harvard has hosted **MILK DAYS** every June, a dairy festival that includes milk drinking for all ages.

In Mount Pulaski, it is illegal for boys to hurl **SNOWBALLS** at trees.

Girls can do as they please.

The Sears Tower in Chicago is the country's **TALLEST** building, at 1,450 feet, 1,729 feet including the spires.

Lockport stipulates that anyone who starts a **DOGFIGHT** by word or gesture will be fined.

Put 'em up?

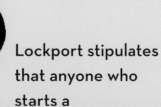

47

IOWA
Hawkeye State

★ **DES MOINES**

Can I have another ear?

Why? You already have two.

Don't be so corny, Dad.

Enough already!

Iowa is one of the country's largest **CORN** producers.

Strawberry Point is home of the world's largest **STRAWBERRY.**

Yum!

Did you know . . . that Wilton Candy Kitchen is considered the oldest operating **SODA FOUNTAIN** in the nation? Since 1856.

Indianola is home to the National Balloon Museum and the U.S. Ballooning Hall of Fame. It's an uplifting experience!

In Marshalltown, horses are **FORBIDDEN** to eat fire hydrants.

Now I know why. This tastes terrible!

48

Iowa is the only state with both east and west borders entirely made of water, the Mississippi and Missouri Rivers.

Iowa is the only state name that starts with two vowels!

Snake Alley in Burlington is the **CROOKEDEST** street in the world.

In landlocked Ashland, where there is no open water for miles, there is a **LIGHTHOUSE.**

Hmmmm . . .

A ship! Oh, wait a minute. Never mind.

NEBRASKA
Cornhusker State

Did you hear something?

Nah.

At the Agate Fossil Beds National Monument, you'll find hundreds of animal **BONES** perfectly preserved, including a 20-million-year-old menoceras (a two-horned prehistoric rhinoceros).

Don't miss the Lied Jungle exhibit — the world's largest indoor rainforest — at the Omaha Zoo.

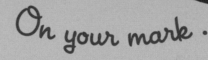

On your mark . . .

Grand Island celebrates the Running of the **WEINERS** Festival every September.

Did you know . . . that every June, Ainsworth hosts a **MIDDLE-OF-NOWHERE CELEBRATION.**

Hey, did you know that Kearney is located exactly halfway between Boston and San Francisco?

Nowhere.

NOWHERE

WHERE

Dear, where are you going?

49

OKLAHOMA
Sooner State

★ OKLAHOMA CITY

"The walls and roof were blown away, but the floor remained intact."

"We eventually glided downward, landing safely back on the ground!"

During a **TORNADO** in Ponca City in 1912, a man and his wife were carried into the air while still in their house!

"Charge!"

Did you know . . .

that the **SHOPPING CART** was invented in Ardmore.

It is illegal to wear your **BOOTS** to bed in Oklahoma.

The world's first parking **METER** was installed in Oklahoma City on July 16, 1935.

All yield to the YIELD sign, designed by Clinton Riggs in 1951 and first used in Tulsa.

Oklahoma's state insect is the honeybee.

In Muskogee, no baseball team is allowed to **HIT** the ball over the fence or out of the ballpark.

Pauls Valley hosts the World's Championship Watermelon **SEED SPITTING** Contest.

51

TEXAS
Lone Star State

AUSTIN

The first word spoken by Neil Armstrong from the **MOON** on July 20, 1969, was "Houston."

The state onion is the 1015 sweet onion.

Texas's state flower is the **BLUEBONNET,** named for its color and because it looks like a woman's sunbonnet.

In 1901, the Spindletop oilfield sprayed more than 800,000 barrels of **OIL** into the air in eight days, heralding the birth of the Texas **OIL** industry.

Oil's well that ends well!

Yee-haw!

Sweetwater is home to the World's Largest **RATTLESNAKE** Roundup.

Did you know . . .

that Hidalgo boasts a twenty-foot-long fiberglass bee as a reminder that, in 1990, the first Africanized **KILLER BEE** crossed into the United States.

FROM U.S.A.

TO U.S.A.

Built in 1870, the Waco Bridge was one of the first **SUSPENSION** bridges in the United States.

Texas hosts the American Institute of Architects **SAND CASTLE** Competition every June.

Glen Rose, now hundreds of miles inland from the Gulf of Mexico, used to be on the shore 113 million years ago. Pleurocoelus and Acrocanthosaurus **DINOSAURS** roamed the area and left their footprints, which are still visible.

A San Antonio law forbids MONKEYS to ride on buses.

53

NEW MEXICO
Land of Enchantment

More than 350,000 **BATS** live in the Carlsbad Caverns.

Did you know . . .

that Lovington hosts the World's Greatest **LIZARD RACE,** where only lizard owners sixteen years old and younger may enter.

Arizona, Colorado, New Mexico, and Utah all meet at **FOUR CORNERS . . .**

AZ

NM

An enormous mud pit with obstacles built just for kids!

Every July, Rio Rancho is home to the Muck in the **MUD** Derby.

The annual **UFO** Encounter Event is held in Roswell, where, in 1947, a number of residents claimed to witness a flying saucer crash.

It's made of 750 pounds of stone-ground corn, 175 gallons of vegetable oil . . .

. . . 75 gallons of red chile sauce, 175 pounds of grated cheese, and 50 pounds of onions.

See the world's largest enchilada in La Cruces at the Whole Enchilada **FIESTA** each September.

Colorado lays claim to the invention of the **CHEESEBURGER** (but so do Kentucky and California).

Rocky Ford is the **SWEET MELON** Capital of the World.

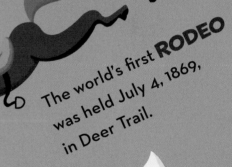

DENVER

Did you know . . . that in Fruita, people celebrate Mike the **HEADLESS CHICKEN** Day.

UT

CO

. . . the only place in the country where four states come together.

Back in 1945, a farmer cut off Mike's head in preparation for a chicken dinner. But Mike lived for another four years without his head!

I lost my head!

The world's first **RODEO** was held July 4, 1869, in Deer Trail.

It is illegal to let a dandelion grow within the city limits in Pueblo.

Boulder is the only U.S. city that has a **GLACIER.**

It is against the law to graze a **LLAMA** on city property in Boulder.

SOUTH DAKOTA
Mount Rushmore State

PIERRE

Get mashed at the **MASHED POTATO WRESTLING** Contest, held annually in Clark.

Mitchell has the world's only **CORN** Palace, where thousands of bushels of **CORN** and grasses create **CORN** murals.

That place is real corny!

See the world's largest exhibit of Columbian **MAMMOTH FOSSILS** at Mammoth Site in Hot Springs.

No eating the exhibits, please.

Did you know . . .
that you can enjoy the **WATERSLIDES**, Tarzan rings, and fun tubes at Evans Plunge.

The world's largest natural warm-water indoor swimming pool is in Hot Springs.

Lie down and fall asleep in a **CHEESE** factory in South Dakota, and you might be arrested!

Aahh!

Visit the four most famous guys in rock—at Mount Rushmore!

Washington!

Jefferson!

Roosevelt!

Lincoln!

56

You will find all things **BUFFALO** at the National Buffalo Museum in Jamestown.

NORTH DAKOTA
Peace Garden State

★ **BISMARCK**

Dunseith is home to the International Old-Time **FIDDLERS** Contest!

In Fargo, you can be imprisoned for wearing a hat while **DANCING,** or even for wearing a hat to a function where dancing is taking place.

Talk about strict!

Do-si-do!

Dear, can you play the North Dakota Hymn? It's the state song.

According to legend, the piles of rock on White Butte, North Dakota's highest point, were piled there by shepherds as a way to pass the time.

Baa, I say!

Did you know . . .
that Rutland was host and chef to the cooking and eating of the **WORLD'S LARGEST HAMBURGER?** In 1982, 8 to 10 thousand people came to have a bite of the delicious 3,591-pound burger.

HOLD THE ONIONS!

MONTANA
Treasure State

Holy cow!

Did you know . . . that there are three head of **CATTLE** for each person in Montana!

You are not allowed to draw **FUNNY FACES** on your window shades in Garfield County.

In Billings, police will confiscate a **PEA SHOOTER'S** shooter if they shoot it! *Say that three times fast!*

Ooof!

LOOK OUT!

The largest **SNOWFLAKE** ever reported was 15 inches wide and fell on January 28, 1887, in Fort Keogh!

Anaconda features one of the largest freestanding brick structures in the world, a 585-foot **SMOKESTACK** known as the Big Stack.

WHOA!

Follow the Montana Dinosaur Trail, made up of 15 museums and field stations across the state.

Don't miss Yellowstone National **PARK.** It was the country's first national park, and it's so big that it's in Montana . . .

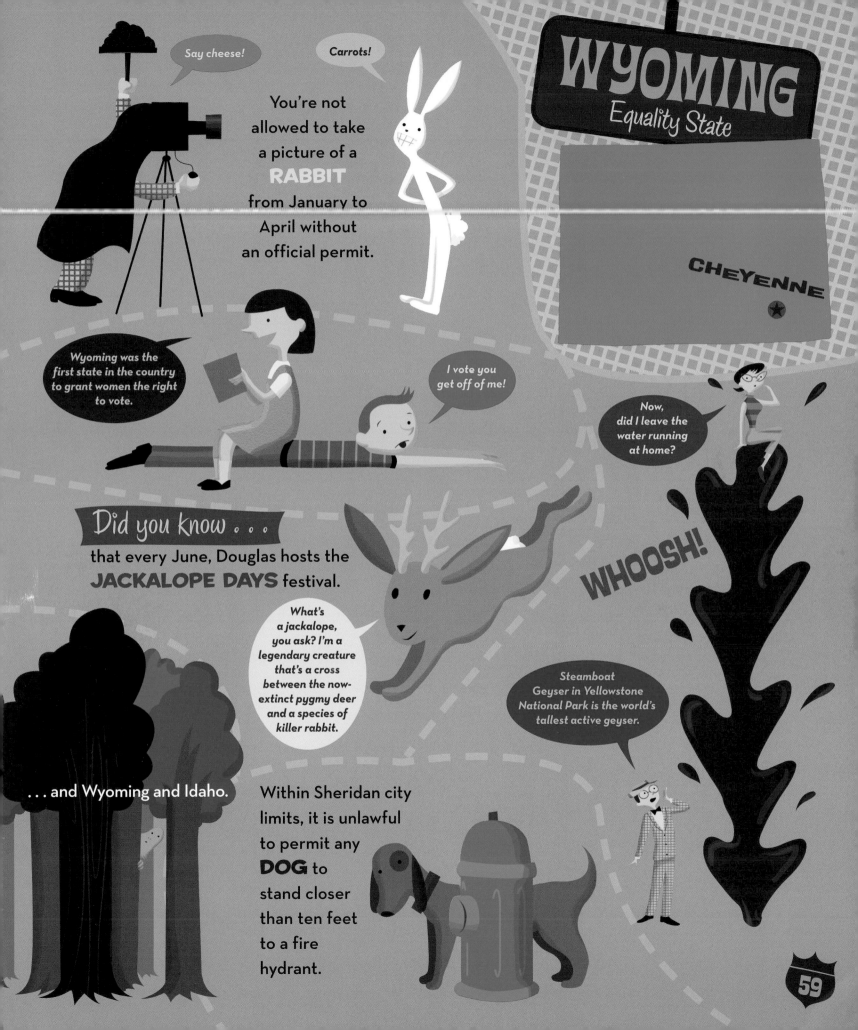

IDAHO
Gem State

★ BOISE

Located in the Nez Perce National Forest, Snake River Canyon is the deepest gorge in the United States.

It has a vertical drop of about 8,000 feet. Watch your step!

Don't fish from the back of a **CAMEL** in Idaho, or you'll be a lawbreaker!

In Pocatello, a person may not be seen in public without a smile on their face.

Idaho's state fruit is the **HUCKLEBERRY**, a favorite with the bears.

Boiled? Mashed? Baked? French-fried?

In Idaho, you may not give your sweetheart a box of **CANDY** that weighs less than 50 pounds!

Did you know . . . that Idaho grows more **POTATOES** a year than anywhere else in the country.

That's one long walk down the block!

The **LONGEST** Main Street in America — 35 miles — is in Island Park.

Boo!

Nevada has hundreds of **GHOST TOWNS.**

Nevada is the gambling capital of the United States. I bet you didn't know that.

Las Vegas is home to the Vegas **VENTRILOQUIST** Convention every June.

Hard hats were first invented for workers on the Hoover Dam in 1933. Now that's using your head!

Did you know that the Hoover Dam contains 3.2 million cubic yards of concrete? At peak production, one bucket of concrete was poured every 78 seconds!

Where are we?

Did you know . . .

that Virginia City hosts the International **CAMEL** Races every September.

Nevada is the driest state in the nation, with an average annual rainfall of only about seven inches!

AND THEY'RE OFF!

In Death Valley, **KANGAROO RATS** don't have to drink even a drop of liquid to survive. They make their own water when they digest seeds.

61

UTAH
Beehive State

In Utah, you may not hire **TROMBONE** players to play on the street to advertise an auction.

Peep! Peep!

Arizona, Colorado, New Mexico, and Utah all meet at **FOUR CORNERS . . .**

CO

UT

Don't miss the **BELLY DANCE** Festival in Kismet every August.

Levan is "navel" spelled backward — perhaps because it's in the middle of Utah.

Read on!

Utah has the **HIGHEST** literacy rate in the nation.

Salt Lake City is home to the nation's leading manufacturer of **RUBBER CHICKENS.**

In Utah, birds have the right of way on all highways.

Did you know . . .

that in Salt Lake County, it's illegal to walk down the street carrying a **PAPER BAG** containing a violin.

The bolo tie is the official state neckwear! Yee-haw!

ARIZONA
Grand Canyon State

NM

AZ

. . . the only place in the country where four states come together.

Did you know . . .

that the town of Why, Arizona, got its name

WHY

from a **Y-SHAPED** intersection of two state highways.

PHOENIX

With almost 332 days of **SUNSHINE** a year, Yuma is the world's sunniest place.

In Oatman every July, there is a **SIDEWALK EGG-FRYING CHALLENGE,** where eggs are fried on hot sidewalks.

YOU MAY NOT WANT TO EAT THEM.

Chandler hosts an annual **OSTRICH** festival every March.

The original London Bridge was shipped stone by stone and reconstructed in Lake Havasu City.

CALIFORNIA
Golden State

★ SACRAMENTO

On Market Street in San Francisco, the law requires **ELEPHANTS** to be kept on a leash.

In California, a toll gatherer may prevent any animal that has not paid the toll from passing through the tollgate or toll bridge.

Two out of three?

California law states that wrestlers may not make faces during the practice of their art.

Did you know . . .

that a Belvedere city council order reads: No **DOG** shall be in a public place without a master on a leash.

Petaluma hosts the World's **WRISTWRESTLING** Championship every October.

No wonder it's called the artichoke, avocado, tomatillo, carrot, and garlic capital of the world!

Eat your vegetables!

Farmers in California grow more than half of all the fruits, vegetables, and **NUTS** in the United States.

California lays claim to the invention of the **CHEESEBURGER** (but so do Kentucky and Colorado).

Hacienda Heights hosts the biggest Fancy **RAT AND MOUSE** Show, every January. *Don't miss it.*

From October 3, 1912, through November 8, 1914, it didn't rain once in Bagdad, California.

The **HIGHEST TEMPERATURE** ever recorded in the United States was 134°F at Greenland Ranch in Death Valley on July 10, 1913.

The lowest and highest points in the continental U.S. are both in California, and just 85 miles apart.

See the bones of ice age animals at the La Brea Tar Pits in Los Angeles!

Chico is the home of the National **YO-YO** Museum.

To find the world's **TALLEST** trees, go to the coast Redwoods at Humboldt Redwoods State Park.

OREGON
Beaver State

SALEM ★

There are a lot of Bigfoot sightings in the woods of Oregon.

Keep your eyes peeled.

Freddie, what's that dripping out of your pocket?

Did not.

In Deschutes County, **BROTHERS** and **SISTERS** can visit a community named Brothers and another named Sisters.

Kids! Brothers and sisters need to get along.

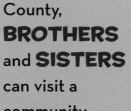

Mom, Freddie stole my ice cream!

The city of Portland was named by a coin toss. The coin tossers each wanted to name the city for their hometowns back East: Portland, Maine, and Boston, Massachusetts.

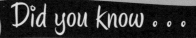

Did you know . . .

that by state law canned corn is not to be used as **BAIT** for fishing!

Seems fishy to me.

Some of the earliest **RHINO FOSSILS** in the world were found in the John Day Fossil Beds National Monument.

There have been many **BIGFOOT** sightings in Washington State, too.

WASHINGTON
Evergreen State

Eatonville hosts the annual **SLUG** festival, where several of Washington's 23 species of slugs are put on display.

The state of Washington is the only state to be named after a U.S. president. Wow!

NO NEED TO HURRY.

Seattle is home to the Space Needle, built for the World's Fair of 1962 and featuring a revolving restaurant at its top!

The snowiest town in the U.S. is Stampede Pass.

Next stop, City Aquarium.

It is unlawful for **GOLDFISH** to ride on a Seattle bus, unless they lie still.

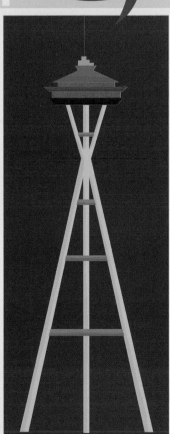

Did you know . . .

that Washington state produces more **APPLES** than any other state, about 5.9 billion pounds per year!

The cloudiest town in the U.S. is Quillayute.

ALASKA
Last Frontier

JUNEAU

The state of Rhode Island could fit into Alaska 425 times!

Ladies and gentlemen, start your tubs . . .

Did you know . . . that every Labor Day, Nome stages the Great American **BATHTUB RACE.**

Hurry before it melts!

Fairbanks hosts the World **ICE ART** Championships every March.

In the old gold rush days, most men were scraggly with large amounts of hair. Maybe it kept them warm.

It's against the law to wake a sleeping **BEAR** in order to photograph it.

First prize goes to the **HAIRIEST** at Alaska's Hairy Chest, Legs, and Beard Contest.

68

It's against the law to look at a moose from an airplane.

During the summer, the sun shines more than 20 hours a day!

The **YETI,** Bigfoot's cousin, supposedly lives in the frozen north.

Do you have your sunglasses, dear?

Mount Denali rises 20,320 feet above sea level and is the **HIGHEST PEAK** in North America!

Feel free to yodel.

One in 58 Alaskans is a **PILOT.**

Alaska is the northernmost and westernmost state of the United States. It's also the largest.

Alaska's state mineral is gold and its state sport is dog mushing.

Alaska was purchased from Russia in 1867 for **7.2 MILLION DOLLARS,** less than two cents an acre.

Eureka!

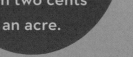

GOLD was discovered in the Klondike region of Alaska in 1896.

HAWAII
Aloha State

★ HONOLULU

Hawaii is the only state that grows coffee.

that in Hawaii, **COINS** are not allowed to be placed in one's ears.

From east to west, Hawaii is the widest state in the United States.

Hawaii is the only island state, and the southernmost state in the United States.

Hawaii is 2,390 miles from California, 3,850 miles from Japan, 4,900 miles from China, and 5,280 miles from the Philippines!

Good thing we have phones.

Cowabunga!

Hawaii is world renowned for its **SURFING!**

Mount Kilauea is one of the most active volcanoes on Earth. Watch out!

Don't forget your galoshes.

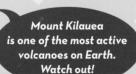

Mount Waialeale, on the island of Kauai, is the **WETTEST** place in the world. An average of 460 inches of rain falls per year, but in 1982, a world record was set with 666 inches!

70

Every April, the island of Hilo holds the World's Largest **HULA** Competition.

Hawaii produces only about 2 percent of the world's pineapples.

Oahu hosts the World's Greatest **LIFEGUARD** Contest.

The **PAPER AIRPLANE** Museum in Kahului has more than 2,000 models from around the world. They range from postage-stamp size to wingspans of more than six feet.

AL	**AK**	**AZ**	**AR**	**CA**	**CO**
ALABAMA	**ALASKA**	**ARIZONA**	**ARKANSAS**	**CALIFORNIA**	**COLORADO**
CAPITAL Montgomery	**CAPITAL** Juneau	**CAPITAL** Phoenix	**CAPITAL** Little Rock	**CAPITAL** Sacramento	**CAPITAL** Denver
STATEHOOD December 14, 1819	**STATEHOOD** January 3, 1959	**STATEHOOD** February 14, 1912	**STATEHOOD** June 15, 1836	**STATEHOOD** September 9, 1850	**STATEHOOD** August 1, 1876
ORDER OF STATEHOOD 22	**ORDER OF STATEHOOD** 49	**ORDER OF STATEHOOD** 48	**ORDER OF STATEHOOD** 25	**ORDER OF STATEHOOD** 31	**ORDER OF STATEHOOD** 38
SQUARE MILES 52,419	**SQUARE MILES** 663,267	**SQUARE MILES** 113,998	**SQUARE MILES** 53,179	**SQUARE MILES** 163,696	**SQUARE MILES** 104,094
BIRD Yellowhammer	**BIRD** Willow ptarmigan	**BIRD** Cactus wren	**BIRD** Mockingbird	**BIRD** California Valley quail	**BIRD** Lark bunting
FLOWER Camellia	**FLOWER** Forget-me-not	**FLOWER** Saguaro cactus blossom	**FLOWER** Apple blossom	**FLOWER** Golden poppy	**FLOWER** Rocky Mountain columbine
TREE Longleaf pine	**TREE** Sitka spruce	**TREE** Yellow paloverde	**TREE** Pine	**TREE** Redwood	**TREE** Blue spruce
MOTTO *Audemus jura nostra defendere* (Latin for "We dare defend our rights")	**MOTTO** North to the future	**MOTTO** *Ditat deus* (Latin for "God enriches")	**MOTTO** *Regnat populus* (Latin for "The people rule")	**MOTTO** *Eureka!* (Greek for "I have found it!")	**MOTTO** *Nil sine numine* (Latin for "Nothing without providence")
NICKNAME Yellowhammer State, Heart of Dixie	**NICKNAME** Last Frontier, Land of the Midnight Sun	**NICKNAME** Grand Canyon State, Copper State	**NICKNAME** Natural State	**NICKNAME** Golden State	**NICKNAME** Centennial State, Colorful Colorado

The Farley family photo gallery:
Can you remember where the Farleys frolicked?

CT	DE	FL	GA	HI	ID
CONNECTICUT	**DELAWARE**	**FLORIDA**	**GEORGIA**	**HAWAII**	**IDAHO**

CAPITAL	**CAPITAL**	**CAPITAL**	**CAPITAL**	**CAPITAL**	**CAPITAL**
Hartford	Dover	Tallahassee	Atlanta	Honolulu	Boise
STATEHOOD	**STATEHOOD**	**STATEHOOD**	**STATEHOOD**	**STATEHOOD**	**STATEHOOD**
January 9, 1788	December 7, 1787	March 3, 1845	January 2, 1788	August 21, 1959	July 3, 1890
ORDER OF STATEHOOD	**ORDER OF STATEHOOD**	**ORDER OF STATEHOOD**	**ORDER OF STATEHOOD**	**ORDER OF STATEHOOD**	**ORDER OF STATEHOOD**
5	1	27	4	50	43
SQUARE MILES	**SQUARE MILES**	**SQUARE MILES**	**SQUARE MILES**	**SQUARE MILES**	**SQUARE MILES**
5,543	2,489	65,755	59,425	10,932	83,570
BIRD	**BIRD**	**BIRD**	**BIRD**	**BIRD**	**BIRD**
Robin	Blue hen chicken	Mockingbird	Brown thrasher	Nene (Hawaiian goose)	Mountain bluebird
FLOWER	**FLOWER**	**FLOWER**	**FLOWER**	**FLOWER**	**FLOWER**
Mountain laurel	Peach blossom	Orange blossom	Cherokee rose	Hibiscus	Syringa
TREE	**TREE**	**TREE**	**TREE**	**TREE**	**TREE**
White oak	American holly	Sabal palm	Live oak	Kukui (Candlenut)	Western white pine
MOTTO	**MOTTO**	**MOTTO**	**MOTTO**	**MOTTO**	**MOTTO**
Qui transtulit sustinet (Latin for "He who transplanted still sustains")	Liberty and independence	In God we trust	Wisdom, justice, and moderation	*Ua mau ke ea o ka aina i ka pono* (Hawaiian for "The life of the land is perpetuated in righteousness")	*Esto perpetua* (Latin for "It is forever")
NICKNAME	**NICKNAME**	**NICKNAME**	**NICKNAME**		**NICKNAME**
Constitution State, Nutmeg State	First State, Diamond State, Blue Hen State, Small Wonder	Sunshine State	Peach State		Gem State
				NICKNAME	
				Aloha State	

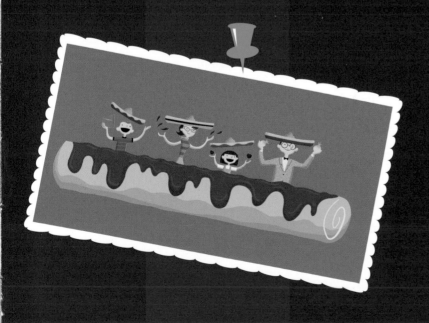

IL	IN	IA	KS	KY	LA
ILLINOIS	**INDIANA**	**IOWA**	**KANSAS**	**KENTUCKY**	**LOUISIANA**

CAPITAL	**CAPITAL**	**CAPITAL**	**CAPITAL**	**CAPITAL**	**CAPITAL**
Springfield	Indianapolis	Des Moines	Topeka	Frankfort	Baton Rouge
STATEHOOD	**STATEHOOD**	**STATEHOOD**	**STATEHOOD**	**STATEHOOD**	**STATEHOOD**
December 3, 1818	December 11, 1816	December 28, 1846	January 29, 1861	June 1, 1792	April 30, 1812
ORDER OF STATEHOOD	**ORDER OF STATEHOOD**	**ORDER OF STATEHOOD**	**ORDER OF STATEHOOD**	**ORDER OF STATEHOOD**	**ORDER OF STATEHOOD**
21	19	29	34	15	18
SQUARE MILES	**SQUARE MILES**	**SQUARE MILES**	**SQUARE MILES**	**SQUARE MILES**	**SQUARE MILES**
57,914	36,418	56,272	82,277	40,409	51,840
BIRD	**BIRD**	**BIRD**	**BIRD**	**BIRD**	**BIRD**
Cardinal	Cardinal	Eastern goldfinch	Western meadowlark	Cardinal	Eastern brown pelican
FLOWER	**FLOWER**	**FLOWER**	**FLOWER**	**FLOWER**	**FLOWER**
Purple violet	Peony	Wild rose	Sunflower	Goldenrod	Magnolia
TREE	**TREE**	**TREE**	**TREE**	**TREE**	**TREE**
White oak	Tulip	Oak	Cottonwood	Tulip poplar	Bald cypress
MOTTO	**MOTTO**	**MOTTO**	**MOTTO**	**MOTTO**	**MOTTO**
State sovereignty, national union	The crossroads of America	Our liberties we prize, and our rights we will maintain	*Ad astra per aspera* (Latin for "To the stars through difficulties")	United we stand, divided we fall	Union, justice, and confidence
NICKNAME	**NICKNAME**			**NICKNAME**	**NICKNAME**
Prairie State	Hoosier State	**NICKNAME**	**NICKNAME**	Bluegrass State	Pelican State
		Hawkeye State	Sunflower State, Jayhawk State		

ME	MD	MA	MI	MN	MS
MAINE	**MARYLAND**	**MASSACHUSETTS**	**MICHIGAN**	**MINNESOTA**	**MISSISSIPPI**

CAPITAL Augusta	**CAPITAL** Annapolis	**CAPITAL** Boston	**CAPITAL** Lansing	**CAPITAL** St. Paul	**CAPITAL** Jackson
STATEHOOD March 15, 1820	**STATEHOOD** April 28, 1788	**STATEHOOD** February 6, 1788	**STATEHOOD** January 26, 1837	**STATEHOOD** May 11, 1858	**STATEHOOD** December 10, 1817
ORDER OF STATEHOOD 23	**ORDER OF STATEHOOD** 7	**ORDER OF STATEHOOD** 6	**ORDER OF STATEHOOD** 26	**ORDER OF STATEHOOD** 32	**ORDER OF STATEHOOD** 20
SQUARE MILES 35,385	**SQUARE MILES** 12,407	**SQUARE MILES** 10,555	**SQUARE MILES** 96,716	**SQUARE MILES** 86,939	**SQUARE MILES** 48,430
BIRD Chickadee	**BIRD** Baltimore oriole	**BIRD** Chickadee	**BIRD** Robin	**BIRD** Common loon	**BIRD** Mockingbird
FLOWER White pine cone and tassel	**FLOWER** Black-eyed Susan	**FLOWER** Mayflower	**FLOWER** Apple blossom	**FLOWER** Pink-and-white lady's slipper	**FLOWER** Magnolia
TREE White pine	**TREE** White oak	**TREE** American elm	**TREE** Eastern white pine	**TREE** Red pine	**TREE** Magnolia
MOTTO *Dirigo* (Latin for "I lead")	**MOTTO** *Fatti maschii, parole femine* (Italian for "Manly deeds, womanly words" or "Strong deeds, gentle words")	**MOTTO** *Ense petit placidam sub libertate quietem* (Latin for "By the sword we seek peace, but peace only under liberty")	**MOTTO** *Si quaeris peninsulam amoenam, circumspice* (Latin for "If you seek a pleasant peninsula, look about you")	**MOTTO** *L'Étoile du nord* (French for "The north star")	**MOTTO** *Virtute et armis* (Latin for "By valor and arms")
NICKNAME Pine Tree State	**NICKNAME** Old Line State, Free State	**NICKNAME** Bay State, Old Colony State	**NICKNAME** Wolverine State, Great Lakes State	**NICKNAME** North Star State, Land of 10,000 Lakes	**NICKNAME** Magnolia State

MO	**MT**	**NE**	**NV**	**NH**	**NJ**
MISSOURI	MONTANA	NEBRASKA	NEVADA	NEW HAMPSHIRE	NEW JERSEY

CAPITAL Jefferson City	**CAPITAL** Helena	**CAPITAL** Lincoln	**CAPITAL** Carson City	**CAPITAL** Concord	**CAPITAL** Trenton
STATEHOOD August 10, 1821	**STATEHOOD** November 8, 1889	**STATEHOOD** March 1, 1867	**STATEHOOD** October 31, 1864	**STATEHOOD** June 21, 1788	**STATEHOOD** December 18, 1787
ORDER OF STATEHOOD 24	**ORDER OF STATEHOOD** 41	**ORDER OF STATEHOOD** 37	**ORDER OF STATEHOOD** 36	**ORDER OF STATEHOOD** 9	**ORDER OF STATEHOOD** 3
SQUARE MILES 69,704	**SQUARE MILES** 147,042	**SQUARE MILES** 77,354	**SQUARE MILES** 110,560	**SQUARE MILES** 9,351	**SQUARE MILES** 8,722
BIRD Bluebird	**BIRD** Western meadowlark	**BIRD** Western meadowlark	**BIRD** Mountain bluebird	**BIRD** Purple finch	**BIRD** Eastern goldfinch
FLOWER Hawthorn	**FLOWER** Bitterroot	**FLOWER** Goldenrod	**FLOWER** Sagebrush	**FLOWER** Purple lilac	**FLOWER** Violet
TREE Flowering dogwood	**TREE** Ponderosa pine	**TREE** Cottonwood	**TREE** Bristlecone pine	**TREE** White birch	**TREE** Red oak
MOTTO *Salus populi suprema lex esto* (Latin for "The welfare of the people shall be the supreme law")	**MOTTO** *Oro y plata* (Spanish for "Gold and silver")	**MOTTO** Equality before the law	**MOTTO** All for our country	**MOTTO** Live free or die	**MOTTO** Liberty and prosperity
NICKNAME Show Me State	**NICKNAME** Treasure State	**NICKNAME** Cornhusker State, Tree Planters' State	**NICKNAME** Battleborn State, Silver State, Sagebrush State	**NICKNAME** Granite State	**NICKNAME** Garden State

PAGE 33	PAGE 58	PAGE 49	PAGE 61	PAGE 9	PAGE 17

NM
NEW MEXICO

NY
NEW YORK

NC
NORTH CAROLINA

ND
NORTH DAKOTA

OH
OHIO

OK
OKLAHOMA

CAPITAL Santa Fe	**CAPITAL** Albany	**CAPITAL** Raleigh	**CAPITAL** Bismarck	**CAPITAL** Columbus	**CAPITAL** Oklahoma City
STATEHOOD January 6, 1912	**STATEHOOD** July 26, 1788	**STATEHOOD** November 21, 1789	**STATEHOOD** November 2, 1889	**STATEHOOD** March 1, 1803	**STATEHOOD** November 16, 1907
ORDER OF STATEHOOD 47	**ORDER OF STATEHOOD** 11	**ORDER OF STATEHOOD** 12	**ORDER OF STATEHOOD** 39 or 40 (with South Dakota)	**ORDER OF STATEHOOD** 17	**ORDER OF STATEHOOD** 46
SQUARE MILES 121,589	**SQUARE MILES** 54,556	**SQUARE MILES** 53,819	**SQUARE MILES** 70,670	**SQUARE MILES** 44,825	**SQUARE MILES** 69,898
BIRD Roadrunner	**BIRD** Bluebird	**BIRD** Cardinal	**BIRD** Western meadowlark	**BIRD** Cardinal	**BIRD** Scissor-tailed flycatcher
FLOWER Yucca flower	**FLOWER** Rose	**FLOWER** Dogwood	**FLOWER** Wild prairie rose	**FLOWER** Scarlet carnation	**FLOWER** Mistletoe
TREE Piñon	**TREE** Sugar maple	**TREE** Pine	**TREE** American elm	**TREE** Ohio buckeye	**TREE** Redbud
MOTTO *Crescit eundo* (Latin for "It grows as it goes")	**MOTTO** *Excelsior* (Latin for "Ever upward")	**MOTTO** *Esse quam videri* (Latin for "To be, rather than to seem")	**MOTTO** Liberty and union now and forever, one and inseparable	**MOTTO** With God, all things are possible	**MOTTO** *Labor omnia vincit* (Latin for "Labor conquers all things")
NICKNAME Land of Enchantment	**NICKNAME** Empire State	**NICKNAME** Old North State, Tarheel State	**NICKNAME** Peace Garden State, Flickertail State, Roughrider State	**NICKNAME** Buckeye State	**NICKNAME** Sooner State

OR	PA	RI	SC	SD	TN
OREGON	**PENNSYLVANIA**	**RHODE ISLAND**	**SOUTH CAROLINA**	**SOUTH DAKOTA**	**TENNESSEE**

OR — **OREGON**

CAPITAL
Salem

STATEHOOD
February 14, 1859

ORDER OF STATEHOOD
33

SQUARE MILES
98,381

BIRD
Western meadowlark

FLOWER
Oregon grape

TREE
Douglas fir

MOTTO
Alis volat propriis (Latin for "She flies with her own wings")

NICKNAME
Beaver State

PA — **PENNSYLVANIA**

CAPITAL
Harrisburg

STATEHOOD
December 12, 1787

ORDER OF STATEHOOD
2

SQUARE MILES
46,055

BIRD
Ruffed grouse

FLOWER
Mountain laurel

TREE
Hemlock

MOTTO
Virtue, liberty, and independence

NICKNAME
Keystone State

RI — **RHODE ISLAND**

CAPITAL
Providence

STATEHOOD
May 29, 1790

ORDER OF STATEHOOD
13

SQUARE MILES
1,545

BIRD
Rhode Island red hen

FLOWER
Violet

TREE
Red maple

MOTTO
Hope

NICKNAME
Ocean State, Plantation State

SC — **SOUTH CAROLINA**

CAPITAL
Columbia

STATEHOOD
May 23, 1788

ORDER OF STATEHOOD
8

SQUARE MILES
32,020

BIRD
Great Carolina wren

FLOWER
Yellow jessamine

TREE
Cabbage palmetto

MOTTO
Animis opibusque parati (Latin for "Prepared in mind and resources") and *Dum spiro spero* (Latin for "While I breathe, I hope")

NICKNAME
Palmetto State

SD — **SOUTH DAKOTA**

CAPITAL
Pierre

STATEHOOD
November 2, 1889

ORDER OF STATEHOOD
39 or 40 (with North Dakota)

SQUARE MILES
77,116

BIRD
Ring-necked pheasant

FLOWER
Pasque

TREE
Black Hills spruce

MOTTO
Under God the people rule

NICKNAME
Mount Rushmore State, Coyote State

TN — **TENNESSEE**

CAPITAL
Nashville

STATEHOOD
June 1, 1796

ORDER OF STATEHOOD
16

SQUARE MILES
42,143

BIRD
Mockingbird

FLOWER
Iris

TREE
Tulip poplar

MOTTO
Agriculture and commerce

NICKNAME
Volunteer State, Big Bend State, Mother of Southwestern Statesmen

TX	**UT**	**VT**	**VA**	**WA**	**DC**
TEXAS	**UTAH**	**VERMONT**	**VIRGINIA**	**WASHINGTON**	**WASHINGTON, D.C.**
CAPITAL Austin	**CAPITAL** Salt Lake City	**CAPITAL** Montpelier	**CAPITAL** Richmond	**CAPITAL** Olympia	Became the capital of the U.S.A. in 1800
STATEHOOD December 29, 1845	**STATEHOOD** January 4, 1896	**STATEHOOD** March 4, 1791	**STATEHOOD** June 25, 1788	**STATEHOOD** November 11, 1889	**STATEHOOD** –
ORDER OF STATEHOOD 28	**ORDER OF STATEHOOD** 45	**ORDER OF STATEHOOD** 14	**ORDER OF STATEHOOD** 10	**ORDER OF STATEHOOD** 42	**ORDER OF STATEHOOD** –
SQUARE MILES 168,581	**SQUARE MILES** 84,899	**SQUARE MILES** 9,615	**SQUARE MILES** 42,774	**SQUARE MILES** 71,300	**SQUARE MILES** 68
BIRD Mockingbird	**BIRD** California gull	**BIRD** Hermit thrush	**BIRD** Cardinal	**BIRD** Willow goldfinch	**BIRD** Wood thrush
FLOWER Bluebonnet	**FLOWER** Sego lily	**FLOWER** Red clover	**FLOWER** American dogwood	**FLOWER** Coast rhododendron	**FLOWER** American Beauty rose
TREE Pecan	**TREE** Blue spruce	**TREE** Sugar maple	**TREE** American dogwood	**TREE** Western hemlock	**TREE** Scarlet oak
MOTTO Friendship	**MOTTO** Industry	**MOTTO** Freedom and unity	**MOTTO** *Sic semper tyrannis* (Latin for "Thus always to tyrants")	**MOTTO** *Alki* (Native American word for "By and by")	**MOTTO** *Justitia Omnibus* (Latin for "Justice for all")
NICKNAME Lone Star State	**NICKNAME** Beehive State	**NICKNAME** Green Mountain State	**NICKNAME** Old Dominion State, Mother State	**NICKNAME** Evergreen State	**NICKNAME** D.C., Nation's Capital

WV	WI	WY
WEST VIRGINIA	WISCONSIN	WYOMING

WEST VIRGINIA	WISCONSIN	WYOMING
CAPITAL Charleston	**CAPITAL** Madison	**CAPITAL** Cheyenne
STATEHOOD June 20, 1863	**STATEHOOD** May 29, 1848	**STATEHOOD** July 10, 1890
ORDER OF STATEHOOD 35	**ORDER OF STATEHOOD** 30	**ORDER OF STATEHOOD** 44
SQUARE MILES 24,231	**SQUARE MILES** 65,498	**SQUARE MILES** 97,814
BIRD Cardinal	**BIRD** Robin	**BIRD** Western meadowlark
FLOWER Rhododendron	**FLOWER** Wood violet	**FLOWER** Indian paintbrush
TREE Sugar maple	**TREE** Sugar maple	**TREE** Cottonwood
MOTTO *Montani semper liberi* (Latin for "Mountaineers are always free")	**MOTTO** Forward	**MOTTO** Equal rights
NICKNAME Mountain State	**NICKNAME** Badger State	**NICKNAME** Equality State

HOME SWEET HOME!

WHERE'D ALL THESE WACKY FACTS COME FROM?

Many, many, many books and websites were consulted in the course of making this book. I estimate it in the hundreds. As you might imagine, doing the research was fascinating, sometimes unbelievable, but always fun. So, where did it all come from? A great deal of the information came from books. Lots and lots of books. Below are some of the most helpful:

BOCK, JUDY, AND RACHEL KRANZ.
Scholastic Encyclopedia of the United States.
New York: Scholastic, 1997.

FRIEDMAN, JAN. *Eccentric America.*
Bucks, England: Bradt Travel Guides, 2001.

HYMAN, DICK. *Crazy Laws.*
New York: Scholastic, 1978.

HYMAN, DICK. *More Crazy Laws.*
New York: Scholastic, 1992.

KANE, JOSEPH NATHAN. *Famous First Facts: A Record of First Happenings, Discoveries, and Inventions in American History.*
New York: H.W. Wilson, 1997.

KIRBY, DOUG, KEN SMITH, AND MIKE WILKINS.
The New Roadside America. New York: Simon & Schuster, 1992.

RUBEL, DAVID. *Scholastic Atlas of the United States.*
New York: Scholastic, 2003.

SEULING, BARBARA. *Wacky Laws.*
New York: Scholastic, 1997.

SEULING, BARBARA. *More Wacky Laws.*
New York: Scholastic, 1998.

TAYLOR, NELSON. *America Bizarro.*
New York: St. Martin's Press, 2000.

In addition, much information came from websites sponsored by each state, its Department of Tourism, and its local governments. Links to most of these sites can be found at the U.S. government's official web portal:

http://www.usa.gov/Agencies/State_and_Territories.shtml
(links to state websites)

http://www.usa.gov/Agencies/Local_Government/Cities.shtml
(links to local government websites)

http://www.usa.gov/Citizen/Topics/Travel_Tourism/State_Tourism.shtml
(links to state tourism websites)

BIG THANKS!

Big huge ginormous thanks to all the folks whose efforts went into the making of this book: Ted Ashley and Jackie Glasthal for their invaluable and exhaustive research. Karen VanRossem and Julie Masters at the Scholastic Library for their indispensable guidance and assistance with the research, and so many little things. Donna Slawsky for her impeccable and much-appreciated fact-checking. Janna Morishima for starting the journey. Marijka Kostiw for her superior art direction. Kristina Albertson for her dazzling design. Leslie Budnick for her expert editing abilities as well as her tireless efforts in map-reading and settling backseat arguments.
And an especially great big thanks to Adrian Thatcher for all of his incredible talent, computer wizardry, and general brilliance.